Barragán
Outside
Barragán

Barragan Foundation

Barragán
Outside
Barragán

A journey through books, trips,
exhibitions and friendships

Vitra
Design
Museum

Contents

Foreword

This publication is based on an illustrated talk presented by Fernanda Canales in June 2024 at the Vitra Design Museum in Weil am Rhein, Germany, as part of the Barragán Lecture series. It puts a focus on the Mexican architect Luis Barragán (1902–1988), whose work has a permanent place in the canon of twentieth-century architecture and continues to fascinate architectural scholars, connoisseurs and enthusiasts.

In her lecture, Fernanda Canales deftly interwove Barragán's biography with his major built works, which are shaped by a skilful approach to spatial and chromatic atmospheres and environments. Following the traces found in his extensive private library, his travels, the exhibitions he saw and his personal and professional friendships, she took the audience on a multi-faceted journey through space and time, conveying a concentrated overview of Barragán's creative work from the late 1920s into the 1980s.

This highly engaging and informative presentation at the Vitra Design Museum provided the impulse to transform the manuscript and related illustrative materials into a publication. As part of this process, we felt that it was important to retain the character of a personally narrated viewpoint in the published content. It is our hope that these efforts reach an interested and appreciative readership.

Our friendly and fruitful relationship with Fernanda Canales goes back many years. We would like to express our sincere thanks to the author for her valuable insights into the work of Luis Barragán. We are also grateful to the other individuals who contributed to the realization of this publication.

MARTIN JOSEPHY
Curator, Barragan Foundation

FERNANDA CANALES

A journey through books, trips, exhibitions and friendships

[01]

Looking at Barragán's main influences enables us to unveil what he saw, read and imagined, and to understand how that was then transformed into built form. I propose a journey guided by Barragán's saying: "Don't try to do what I do: see what I saw."[1] We will briefly observe the world that surrounded Barragán and pay special attention to what was happening in architecture at the time, in order to comprehend where the main ideas were coming from. We will look outside Barragán in order to look inward. Following his steps, we will focus on four topics that were his main sources of inspiration: his books, trips, exhibitions, and friends or collaborators.

For Barragán, riding a horse was in equal parts sitting on a horse and dressing up, using the lexicons specific to those activities, and even enjoying breakfast as part of the ritual of riding. Everything that was around him — be it the landscape or a watering trough — was not treated as a background and never as a set of separated elements, but as

[02]   [03]

linked parts with no division between objects, sounds, activities, spaces, emotions and nature. Likewise, architecture was a carefully crafted ritual encompassing all things: from the echo produced by walking across a wooden floor and then abruptly cancelled by a carpet, slowing you down before entering into a garden; to a cave-like space that presses in on you before the discovery of a staircase that becomes a golden vacuum, sweeping you to an upper-floor terrace [→ 01, 02, 03]. In many ways, visiting Barragán's

[1] Raúl Rispa, *Barragán: The Complete Works*, New York, 1996, p. 21.

9

[04]

work is visiting the cities where he travelled, the gardens he saw, the books he cherished, as well as meeting his collaborators.

Seeing – through the eyes of Barragán – is absorbing everything, turning sounds into music, gardens into introspection, books into worlds. Therefore, the intention is to understand what was in his hands in order to fully grasp his legacy. Our aim is not only to trace the references he purposefully left us, following the breadcrumbs he carefully placed like Hansel and Gretel, but also to look at the other side of the things that were there, right in front of him, that must have been impossible to miss. This is neither a detective's speculation nor a psychological analysis, but a framework that can contextualize his work.

This journey is divided into four periods, based on four trips to Europe that Barragán undertook during his lifetime, which defined the particularities of his work during each era. The trips are a guideline, apertures for viewing the four periods: the first, in the mid 1920s, when

[05]

he developed his initial projects in Guadalajara under the impression of the Mediterranean tradition; the second, during the 1930s, when he moved to Mexico City and designed some of the first buildings in Latin America in the International Style; the third period, during the 1940s and '50s, when he established the style for which he is recognized today; and the fourth and last phase, in the 1960s and '70s, culminating in his late masterpiece, the Gilardi House, and the exhibition of his work at the

[06]

[07]

Museum of Modern Art in New York in 1976. Each of these four periods is defined by the books, texts and friendships that marked their striking differences, as well as by distinct geographies: Guadalajara in the first period; Mexico City's central neighbourhoods in the second; mainly the southern reaches of Mexico City in the third; and mostly areas north of the capital in the fourth.

The primary material for this lecture comes from Barragán's personal library, preserved in his home, where he spent the last forty years of his life [→ 05, 06, 07, 08].[2] Conducting research in this library is akin to encountering a self-portrait of Barragán. He defined his library as being "what helped me [...] to maintain my calling for the architectural profession".[3] So, to find his gaze within so many volumes – around 2,200 books – it is necessary to acknowledge that the library has been touched by many more hands since his death thirty-six years ago. Like any library, things have been moved and affected by random circumstances, such as

[08]

books received as gifts, but it still represents a trustworthy record of what repeatedly influenced and inspired him.[4]

To unwrap the many layers a library holds, it is necessary to not only look at the books, and the books behind the books, but also at the notes inside them. In Barragán's library, forty percent of the books are

[2] Barragán's personal library is held by the Fundación de Arquitectura Tapatía Luis Barragán and is still located in the architect's former house at 14 Calle Francisco Ramírez, Mexico City.
[3] Alejandro Ramírez Ugarte, *Conversación con Luis Barragán*, Guadalajara, 2015, p. 18.
[4] For example, Barragán's library includes the personal library of artist Miguel Covarrubias, bequeathed upon the latter's death. See Alfonso Alfaro,
Voces de tinta dormida: Itinerarios espirituales de Luis Barragán, Mexico City, 1996, pp. 32, 44.

dedicated to art, twenty percent to literature, seventeen percent to architecture, seven percent to history and religion, and the rest to philosophy and archaeology. It is estimated that thirty percent of the volumes contain some kind of annotations by Barragán.[5] So the search encompassed diving inside the books, especially the books on architecture, which until now have paradoxically escaped much notice in a library that has mainly drawn the attention of writers and historians, but not architects.

The four eras are defined as well by the sociopolitical and artistic movements that were prevalent at the time. I will briefly explain the first two phases, which correspond to Barragán's formative years, since they have been widely referenced in publications. Regarding the two last periods, I will place a deeper focus on the books that were the strongest influences during the time when he developed his most important projects.

The first period is when Barragán, who was born in Guadalajara in 1902, took his first trip to Europe at the age of 22 and spent a year-

[09]

[10]

and-a-half there. Having completed his studies in civil engineering in his home town – without ever having visited Mexico City – he initially travelled with a group led by his professor Agustín Basave. Following the latter's advice to pursue his artistic interests, Barragán then set off on his own. Significant destinations on his trip were the Generalife gardens in Granada's Alhambra [→ 09, 10] and the 1925 International Exhibition of Modern Decorative and Industrial Arts in Paris, where he must have

[5] Fernando Curiel Gámez, "La crítica de Barragán hacia la publicidad de la vida moderna y su visión sobre la espiritualidad del arte encarnada en su obra arquitectónica: 1940–1980", in: *ACE, Architecture, City and Environment*, vol. 16, no. 47, p. 4.

seen Le Corbusier's Pavillon de l'Esprit Nouveau [→ 11] and Frederick Kiesler's "City in Space" [→ 12] exhibit. Despite Barragán's assessment that everything in the exhibition was a visual offense, that "he was unable to find a place where his eyes could peacefully rest", he would meet these two figures on his next trip in 1931, and they would always be important references.[6]

At the Paris exhibition, it is likewise probable that he saw the Spanish Pavilion designed by Pascual Bravo [→ 13], a building in the neo-colonial Andalusian style that informed Barragán's work in Guadalajara over the next years. He also discovered a garden designed by Ferdinand Bac, known as the prince of metaphors, author of two books published that year: *Les Colombières* and *Jardins enchantés* (Enchanted Gardens) [→ 14, 15]. Barragán purchased numerous copies of these books and took them home to Guadalajara, distributing seven as gifts to friends such as Ignacio Díaz Morales and Rafael Urzúa, and keeping three copies of *Les Colombières*

 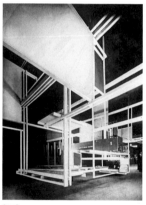 

[11] [12] [13]

and two of *Jardins enchantés* for himself.[7] Along with other books acquired during that trip – particularly on vernacular houses in North Africa and the role of domestic courtyards – these publications were life-changing influences.

[6] Ignacio Díaz Morales, "The Essence of Architectural Space", in: Ignacio San Martin, *Luis Barragán: The Phoenix Papers*, Tempe, Arizona, 1997, p. 49.
[7] Fernando González Gortázar, *Ignacio Díaz Morales habla de Luis Barragán*, Guadalajara, 1991, p. 35.

· FERDINAND · BAC ·

LES
COLOMBIÈRES

SES JARDINS ET SES DÉCORS

COMMENTÉS PAR LEUR AUTEUR

AVEC 60 PLANCHES EN COULEURS

[14]

FERDINAND BAC

JARDINS ENCHANTÉS

UN ROMANCERO

TRENTE-SIX JARDINS EN COULEURS DESSINÉS PAR L'AUTEUR

PARIS
LOUIS CONARD, LIBRAIRE-EDITEUR
6, Place de la Madeleine, 6
—
MCMXXV

[15]

The books by Ferdinand Bac – where literature, art, nature and architecture merge as a unitary sphere – exemplified the pleasure Barragán did not seem to find in his career as a civil engineer, and presented the possibility of building fantasies with no restrictions. The books on the North African house, in turn, made him consider the popular architecture of Mexico within a new hierarchy. All of this broadened his definition of architecture and gave him license to understand the legacy of the past irrespective of historical periods or national borders.

In Mexico, the primary architectural references at the time were either the neoclassical Beaux-Arts buildings made with imported materials, which were characteristic of the Porfirio Díaz regime prior to the Mexican Revolution in 1910 [→ 16], or the post-revolutionary, neo-prehispanic and neo-colonial buildings based on a new national identity [→ 17, 18]. But Barragán instead discovered an endless repertoire, when suddenly the architecture of Mexico was no longer just from that country, but part

[16]

[17]

[18]

of a universal history, shared with the ancient cultures encompassed by the term "Mediterranean".

Back in Guadalajara, Barragán felt liberated from academicism, free to explore the possibilities of the Arab house and its courtyards, to emulate what he found in Bac's books, which contained drawings of a red garden [→ 19], a blue room, a green room, and also phrases that must have resonated with him. For example: "the beauty of a bare wall"; or

"In a garden your eyes plunge into the chimera of the wall to seek in its perspectives a greater joy, and find in the fountains the strange murmur of vanished landscapes."[8] From that point on, patios, fountains, secret gardens, terraces and stairs became primary elements in Barragán's design lexicon.

These influences marked the beginning of a new architectural movement in Guadalajara, developed with two friends from his university days, Díaz Morales and Urzúa, and later referred to by scholars as the Escuela Tapatía. Together they worked on several projects, searching for the essence of things, giving birth to a new regional spirit that emerged in Guadalajara's residential neighbourhoods during the post-revolutionary period, when prominent families were moving from their haciendas and ranches to the safer environment of the city, whose population increased by thirty percent in the 1920s.

The houses designed by Barragán in his native city between 1927 and 1936, such as the Robles León House or the González Luna House [→ 20],

[20]

reflect a proud pursuit of a new local style. In these houses he synthesized his childhood memories of Jalisco's haciendas and colonial convents; of Islamic, Mediterranean and Mexican traditions. His work was closely related to the drawings of Bac's gardens. The most important lessons of Bac were slowly revealed on an abstract level in Barragán's mature work, and the French artist's influence can be summarized in three aspects: the free appropriation of diverse cultures and references; the liberty to

---

[8] Ferdinand Bac, *Les Colombières*, Paris, 1925, pp. 76, 98.

design a space while experiencing and walking through it; and the value of gardens as something no less important than buildings – or even more so. These three qualities propelled Barragán's trajectory towards an architecture with no roof.

The second period began when Barragán, at the age of 29, meanwhile having not only lost his parents but also the family estate Rancho Corrales in Jalisco due to post-revolutionary land reforms, travelled again to Europe in 1931. On the way he stopped in New York, where he spent three months and established a friendship with the Mexican muralist José Clemente Orozco, for whom he later contributed to the designs of two houses and art studios, one in Guadalajara and the other in Mexico City. Barragán also made the acquaintance of Frederick Kiesler, who reportedly gave him a very useful book about the "Dos and Don'ts" of modern architecture.[9]

In 1931, Barragán met Le Corbusier briefly in Paris after seeking

[21]

[22]

out his atelier. He not only ordered all the books Le Corbusier had published, but also visited some of his recently completed works, such as Villa Savoye, Villa Stein [→ 21] and the Beistegui penthouse apartment [→ 22], the latter of which we can see resonating in the Mexican architect's future work. Le Corbusier's description of Villa Stein in a letter to his mother is especially noteworthy: "The garden has become very charming. The house looks centuries old, as it appears so naturally embedded in the

<hr />

[9] Ramírez Ugarte, *Conversación*, 2015, pp. 25–26. In this conversation, held in 1962, Barragán described the book but did not specifically mention its title.

[23]

Puerta en les Colombières
colores rojo, verde, negro y oro (oro = amarillo)
LB - 971

environs."[10] While Barragán's colleagues in Mexico and the United States were looking at the very new, white Corbusian architecture in monochromatic publications, Barragán was physically encountering its timeless qualities and the colourful blues, yellows, pinks and reds of his palette. He experienced Le Corbusier's architecture as a promenade, a ritualized sequence of spaces. In it he also observed the introduction of the exterior into the living spaces, the use of flat roofs as terraces, and the framing of the sky in ways both innovative and reminiscent of the historical courtyards Barragán so admired.

During this trip he also met Ferdinand Bac and visited his recently completed garden and villa in Menton on the French Riviera [→ 24]. Thanks to Bac, Barragán understood the garden not as scenery or a place, but as a protagonist of architecture, and after visiting Le Corbusier's Beistegui Apartment, he must have understood architecture as a stage: a production of feelings composed of light, framed views, sculptural stairs and

[25]

[26]

clouds passing by in the sky. These two encounters, with Le Corbusier and Bac, evidently informed Barragán's statement of what an architect should be: "an artist who manages to dispel anxiety and create illusions".[11] However, after meeting Bac, Barragán wrote how differently they regarded the need to embrace new times. He rejected Bac's withdrawal from modern life, and in that sense felt closer to the principles of the Bauhaus, which he repeatedly cited as an important influence, and closer

[10] Letter from Le Corbusier to his mother, 12 July 1928, Fondation Le Corbusier, FLC-R2(1)11.
[11] Elena Poniatowska, *Todo México*, vol. 1, Mexico City, 1991, p. 26.

to Le Corbusier's book *Vers une architecture* [→ 25], which presented Greek temples next to modern automobiles and juxtaposed the houses in Pompeii with machines and new modern buildings.

While in Europe, Barragán also visited Stuttgart.[12] Although there is no proof that he saw the recently completed buildings from the 1927 Weissenhof exhibition, designed by Mies van der Rohe, Le Corbusier [→ 26] and other pioneers of the modern movement, it is difficult to imagine him – or any other architect visiting Stuttgart at that time – missing such widely published works. Essential features of those houses were honest materials and simple volumes, bright colours, sculptural staircases and rooftop terraces.

Before returning to Mexico, Barragán briefly stopped again in New York, in 1932, missing by just two months the legendary exhibition on Modern Architecture at the Museum of Modern Art, but probably acquiring the catalogue [→ 27], which forms part of his personal library.

[27]   [28]

[29]

It is also possible that he took note of the prior pamphlet *Built to Live In* [→ 28], announcing the museum's plans to mount its first architecture exhibition and prepared in March 1931 by Philip Johnson as an introduction to what would become known as the International Style. It is surely no coincidence that Barragán's work during this second period followed these principles, when he moved to Mexico City in 1935 and built several modern apartment buildings and private villas [→ 23].

[12] Ramírez Ugarte, *Conversación*, 2015, p. 24.

Two friendships that began during the late 1930s came to play a significant role: the first with Richard Neutra, an architect featured in the MoMA catalogue and also in the preceding pamphlet. Neutra, who had emigrated from Austria to the United States and lived in California, visited Mexico in 1937 [→ 29]. The second relationship was with the German architect Max Cetto [→ 30], who first moved to California to work with Neutra and then settled permanently in Mexico in 1939.[13] Cetto would become a key collaborator of Barragán's during this period; together they designed one of the most interesting projects of the time, the artists' apartments in Parque Melchor Ocampo [→ 31].

Cetto and Neutra, after arriving in North America, combined the lessons of the European *Existenzminimum* with the open spirit, temperate climate, lush flora and varied geography of their new environment. Cetto said that in Mexico it was impossible to follow the gridded drawings produced in an office according to strictly functional principles, and that

[30]

[31]

architecture had to change depending on what was found walking across the site – incorporating the richness of the local materials, vegetation, pre-existing conditions and culture.

This tropicalization of the modern movement was characteristic of the architecture in Mexico City in the 1930s, as seen in the work of Juan O'Gorman, especially in the house he designed for his father, as well as the house and studio conceived for the artists Diego Rivera

---

[13] Antonio Ruiz Barbarin, *Luis Barragán frente al espejo*, Madrid, 2008, p. 272.

[32]

and Frida Kahlo [→ 32]. These works, recognized as the first modern houses built by a Latin American architect, manifested a new local spirit rooted in the radical social and artistic movements of the time – propelled by Rivera, Kahlo, Leopoldo Méndez, the members of the Estridentista movement and the Italian photographer Tina Modotti, among others.[14]

Barragán was not part of the social movement in the architecture of the post-revolutionary era, which was vigorously advocated by some of his peers in Mexico City, such as Juan O'Gorman [→ 33], Juan Legarreta, the members of the Union of Socialist Architects, and Hannes Meyer, second director of the Bauhaus who immigrated to Mexico in 1938.[15] This group promoted a socialist agenda and worked through government programmes to build schools, public housing and hospitals. Barragán, on the other hand, who came from an aristocratic background, was searching for the beauty and generous spaces of the haciendas and convents

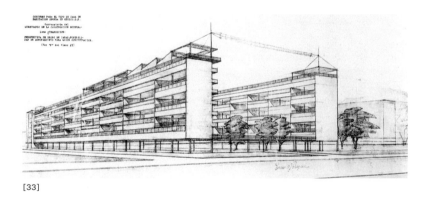

[33]

that had shaped his aesthetic sensibility, while confronted with his new urban life in the capital, which had almost doubled its population in fifteen years. Barragán did not participate in political movements and did not seek to solve the problems of social inequality; rather, he was interested in creating sanctuaries of peace, pleasure and privacy within the changing scenario of a country that was losing the foundation of traditional life valued by conservative groups.

[14] See Fernanda Canales, "Juan O'Gorman: 1905–1982", in: *Letras Libres*, May 2005, pp. 90–91.
[15] See Fernanda Canales, *Architecture in Mexico 1900–2010: The Construction of Modernity*, Mexico City, 2013.

The third period commenced in 1940, when Barragán felt disappointed by the restrictions of his projects and clients, who did not care for architecture beyond its commercial benefits, and decided to abandon the architectural profession. He complained of having to "serve a lot, earn almost nothing, and have many unpleasant moments with clients".[16] So he embarked on his own real estate ventures and focused on the design of gardens. He purchased large parcels of land along Calzada Madereros and in El Cabrío [→ 34], and in 1945 he undertook a development project for a huge expanse of land further south in El Pedregal [→ 35], where he colonized the volcanic landscape and initiated a new architectural style, extending the capital city outside its historical boundaries.

Barragán referred to the liberty he found in the creation of his initial gardens as the factor that spawned his wide recognition. In the gardens of Calzada Madereros he designed a house for himself [→ 36], integrating the remnants of pre-existing structures. Later he sold that

[34]

house to Alfredo Ortega and built a new house and studio for himself on the neighbouring plot, where he lived until his death in 1988 [→ 37].

This period is defined by two texts and four fundamental friendships: with a photographer, a sculptor, a painter and a designer. Barragán's friendship with the photographer Armando Salas Portugal [→ 38] was essential in framing a new gaze. They met in 1944 at an exhibition showcasing Salas Portugal's photographs of the Pedregal lava fields, marking

<hr />

[16] Ramírez Ugarte, *Conversación*, 2015, p. 22.

[35]

[36]

[37]

[38]

the beginning of a collaboration that would continue over the next three decades.[17] His friendship with the German artist and sculptor Mathias Goeritz [→ 39], whom he met in 1949 shortly after Goeritz moved to Mexico, was fundamental, as we can see in the co-authorship of the Torres de Satélite [→ 57]. Similarly consequential was the friendship with the painter Jesús "Chucho" Reyes [→ 40], who would become a project advisor and colour consultant, and with the Cuban-born designer Clara Porset [→ 41], whose furniture appeared in many of his interiors.

During this time, Barragán's library grew considerably. This is when many books found a place in his home, where they remain today. His interest was evidently focused on publications devoted to garden design, especially Japanese gardens, which were pivotal in his work. He also purchased several books on fountains, courtyards, plazas and villas, which found a place on his shelves next to books about painters (from Goya to Giorgio de Chirico), poets and saints.

[39]

[40]

[41]

The two texts from this period that were of particular significance to Barragán's thinking and work were an essay by Diego Rivera, titled "Requirements for the Organization of El Pedregal", and Mathias Goeritz's manifesto on "Emotional Architecture" from 1953.[18]

Rivera's text was the point of departure for the development of El Pedregal, recognizing its potential and proposing a specific approach. The virgin landscape's rough beauty had been previously explored and

[17] See Armando Salas Portugal, "Luis Barragán and His Work", in: San Martin, *Phoenix Papers*, 1997, p. 59.
[18] Ramírez Ugarte, *Conversación*, 2015, p. 47.

captured in images by the painters Dr Atl and Rivera himself, and also by the photographer Salas Portugal. In his text, Rivera articulated guidelines for a place where a new city would emerge, free from the issues of overcrowding, earthquakes and flooding that plagued Mexico City, where modern ideals could flourish while preserving the historical legacy of Mesoamerica, visible in the igneous rocks produced by the eruption of the Xitle volcano two thousand years earlier.

Rivera's ideas were vital for Barragán's design approach to the Jardines del Pedregal subdivision and are clearly reflected in a text the architect wrote in 1944, titled "Some ideas for the development of the residential park El Pedregal de San Angel".[19] Here he outlined the principles of this vast development, where single-family houses would reflect a new paradigm, such as the residence Barragán designed for the Prieto López family [→ 42], two model homes built in collaboration with Max Cetto [→ 43, 45], and houses designed by Francisco Artigas [→ 44], among others.

[42]

[43]

[44]

Goeritz's manifesto on "Emotional Architecture", first presented as a talk at the inauguration of El Eco [→ 46, 47], his experimental museum in Mexico City, was also an essential influence.[20] It strongly advocated for an architecture that put "emotion" at its centre, rejecting the misunderstood and oppressive concept of a functionalism reduced to rational considerations. The document highlighted the need for a "spiritual elevation", through a different way of producing architecture, reclaiming

[19] See Antonio Riggen Martínez, *Luis Barragán: Escritos y conversaciones*, Madrid, 2000, pp. 22–23.
[20] Mathias Goeritz, "Arquitectura Emocional: El Eco", in: *Cuadernos de Arquitectura*, no. 1, March 1954. The manifesto was first presented as a talk at the museum opening in September 1953.

[45]

CUADERNOS DE ARQUITECTURA   **1**   MARZO 1954   ARTES ALIADAS

ARQUITECTURA EMOCIONAL

EL ECO

mathias goeritz

[46]

VISTA AL INTERIOR DEL PATIO

PASILLO DE ENTRADA

[47]

[48]

it as an art form, like the pyramids and Gothic cathedrals. In this essay, Goeritz defined the small patio of his museum as an enclosed and mysterious plaza, and described the building as a narrative based on the sequence of feelings. He wrote that the project had been mainly designed on site, without the use of exact plans, and the same process would occur more and more in Barragán's own designs.

This period culminated in another trip to Europe in 1952, where Barragán spent over a year on sabbatical after selling the Pedregal properties. Following the path of the images found in the book he had discovered on his first trip to Europe, he visited Morocco and the kasbahs (vernacular houses of the Saharan desert) [→ 48], which impressed him more than anything else he had seen on his travels, as he later recounted. [21]

During this time abroad, he also attended the congress of the International Federation of Landscape Architects in Stockholm in 1952. It is highly probable that he visited the Woodland Cemetery and gardens

[49]

[50]

designed by Gunnar Asplund and Sigurd Lewerentz [→ 49], considered one of the most important works of the time and included in the tours offered for conference participants.

A trip to California in 1951 was also crucial for Barragán, where he travelled to showcase his landscape designs in a lecture titled "Gardens for Environment: Jardines del Pedregal" [→ 50]. [22] There he spoke about the "sex appeal" of gardens, and described them as the necessary element

[21] Ramírez Ugarte, *Conversación*, 2015, p. 47.
[22] Lecture held in Coronado, California, on 6 October 1951. Luis Barragán, "Gardens for Environment: Jardines del Pedregal", *Journal of The American Institute of Architects*, no. 4, April 1952, pp. 167–172.

for achieving the mystery and privacy that people need for their personal development. He defined the art of garden design as the main work of humanity in which serenity could be attained.

Over the course of his visit to California, he observed the architecture of Richard Neutra and saw the work of other contemporaries as well. Several notations by Barragán in Neutra's book *Survival Through Design* show how important he found Neutra's ideas. But this trip also made him aware of how differently he viewed the priorities of modern architecture in comparison to Neutra and most of his peers. Barragán particularly lamented the lack of privacy, due to what he considered an excessive use of glass. Additionally, this trip reinforced his appreciation for the strength of contemporary architecture in Mexico. He referred to Mexico as the country with the highest contemporary sensibility and stated that modern architecture in the United States represented only twenty percent of what was being built, while in Mexico it was close to ninety percent,

[51]

[52]

and was part of a new culture encompassing art, music, literature, furniture and landscape design. [23]

At that time, Ciudad Universitaria was about to be completed as the emblem of Mexican modernity, including such works as Juan O'Gorman's Central Library [→ 51], buildings by Mario Pani and Alberto Arai [→ 52], and the Integración Plástica movement, defined by experimentation and the search for a local modern idiom defined by the integration of the arts.

---

[23] Ramírez Ugarte, *Conversación*, 2015, p. 33.

After his trips to California and Europe, Barragán returned to Mexico not only as a widely recognized landscape designer but again as an architect, ready to build the Gálvez House [→55] and the Capuchin Convent in Tlalpan [→ 53, 56]. In the Capuchin Chapel, we can see the influence of Barragán's recurrent visits to the former Jesuit church and college in Tepotzotlán from the seventeenth century [→ 54], located north of Mexico City. It clearly served as a reference in regard to the ways that it evokes light, spiritual elevation, surprise and mystery. The Capuchin Convent is defined by introspection, by a sense of privacy, and by a very different use of glass from what was common at the time, which Barragán consistently criticized.

The fourth and last period corresponds to Barragán's travels to Europe in 1964, undertaken together with his friend Juan Sordo Madaleno to visit the new housing estates in Sweden, Denmark and England, during the time when they were designing the master plan for Lomas

[53]

[54]

Verdes, a satellite community for 100,000 inhabitants north of Mexico City [→ 58, 62]. Barragán and Sordo Madaleno thought of Lomas Verdes as a new city, and this inspired the design of a monumental urban programme encompassing commerce, public spaces, offices and municipal buildings, schools, churches and housing.

Prior to his final European trip, Barragán had worked on the development of Las Arboledas, located north of the Mexican capital,

[55]

[56]

[57]

[58]

where he also designed Los Clubes and Cuadra San Cristóbal [→ 69]. These areas were not far from the Torres de Satélite [→ 57], the landmark and symbol of a modern culture and lifestyle, jointly conceived with Goeritz in 1957.

The books that Barragán purchased during this period mainly dealt with urban planning, public spaces and pedestrian life. One of his primary references was the book *Townscape* by Gordon Cullen [→ 59], published in 1961, which contains copious annotations by the architect. Surely by no coincidence, it focuses on specific lessons and concepts such as "anticipation", "mystery", "intimacy" and "nostalgia". Pages are exclusively dedicated to stairs, shadows, water, quiet enclosures and spatial sequences [→ 60]. Not spaces per se, but spaces as they are revealed, such as the promenades of Le Corbusier or the processional character of Bac's gardens. Cullen calls this "serial vision", describing it as "the gradual unfolding, the encouragement of an intimate atmosphere,

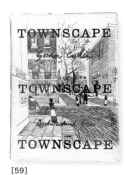

[59]

[60]

[61]

the provision of variety, variety of color and texture, variety of vista and immediacy".[24] Where the user is meant to be indulged.

This approach is a far cry from the Functional City and closer to the predominant references found in Barragán's library, such as books on Antoni Gaudí. After Le Corbusier, the architect Gaudí is represented by the second-largest number of books in Barragán's library. This distance from functionalism is also evident in Barragán's fondness for

---

[24] Gordon Cullen, *Townscape*, London, 1961, p. 257.

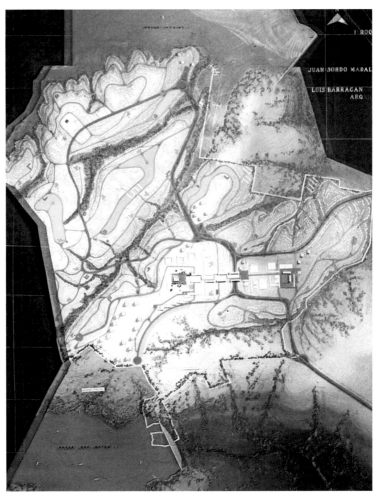

[62]

[63]

Le Corbusier's 1958 publication *Le poème électronique* [→ 61], the book that was lying on his bedside table when he died. [25] It is the least architectural of Le Corbusier's published works, something like a collage of colours, different papers and textures, with abstract photographs of clouds, religious images, ancient sculptures and varied artistic representations.

Also essential for Barragán were two books written by Bernard Rudofsky, as well as two exhibitions curated by the latter. Work by Barragán appeared in Rudofsky's exhibition *Stairs*, presented at Harvard in 1961 and at the New York Museum of Modern Art two years later [→ 63]. In this exhibition, the image of the stairs in Barragán's library was displayed together with photographs of staircases from the Baroque period, ziggurats in the desert, and modern buildings. In a way, the selection illustrated Barragán's fundamental quest for timeless constructions. This discourse came to the forefront of Rudofsky's next MoMA exhibition in 1964, *Architecture Without Architects*, accompanied by a publication

ARCHITECTURE WITHOUT ARCHITECTS
by Bernard Rudofsky

[64]

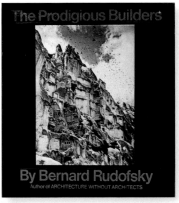

[65]

[66]

with the same title [→ 64], of which three copies are preserved in Barragán's library. A further book by Rudofsky titled *The Prodigious Builders: Notes Toward a Natural History of Architecture* [→ 65] delved deeper into earthbound building traditions and was likewise an important reference for the Mexican architect. Following in this same line is the book *Villages in the Sun: Mediterranean Community Architecture* by Myron Goldfinger [→ 66], also profusely annotated by Barragán.

---

[25] Alfaro, *Voces de tinta dormida*, 1996, p. 84.

During the 1960s, Barragán was shaped by one last important book, friendship and trip. After meeting Josef and Annie Albers – thanks to Clara Porset – during one of the Albers' trips to Mexico, Barragán visited them in 1967 in their studio in Connecticut.[26] Josef's book *Interaction of Color* [→ 68], published in 1963, was a decisive instrument for Barragán. It reveals the wonders of colours, how they interact and communicate with each other, and how our perception of them changes according to different combinations. The book is composed of more than 200 chromatic studies, a sort of bible of colours, similar to the advice Barragán received from painters such as Chucho Reyes.

The two works in which Barragán most freely experimented with colour, Cuadra San Cristóbal [→ 69] and the Gilardi House [→ 70, 71], were completed after his trip to the Albers' studio. That visit also prompted Annie Albers to contact Arthur Drexler, director of the Department of Architecture and Design at MoMA, and suggest that he mount an exhibition

[67]

[68]

of Barragán's work.[27] Curated by Emilio Ambasz, the show opened in 1976 and was accompanied by the first monographic publication on Barragán, which signalled his worldwide recognition, further consolidated in 1980 with the Pritzker Prize.

In 1985, three years prior to his death, Barragán was honoured with a major retrospective at the Museo Tamayo in Mexico City [→ 72, 73]. Prepared by the Barragán + Ferrera office, where Raúl Ferrera was a partner

[26] See Emilia Terragni, "Art Within Architecture", in:
Federica Zanco, *Luis Barragán: The Quiet Revolution*, Milan, 2001, p. 259.
[27] See Riggen Martínez, *Luis Barragán*, 2000, p. 154.

[69]

[70]

[71]

during the final decade of the elder architect's career, the exhibition aimed to convey the way in which Barragán's projects evolved. His method, according to his last collaborator, consisted in developing a "spoken portrait" of the project, as Barragán called it.[28] This phase was more deeply rooted in literature, harking back to Bac and related to the idea of "dreaming" the architecture with a description of the spatial sequences and associated feelings (similar to Goeritz's El Eco manifesto). In the process of conceiving a project, Barragán produced such a description, as if the building already existed. Then the schematic drawing phase took place, discarding, changing, starting again from scratch, until a "thousand alternatives" were considered and the project was finally approved by Barragán. Even then, it continued to change during its construction, especially in the final stage when the colours were defined and tested on site, over and over.[29]

Understanding architecture as a description, as a carefully orchestrated sequence of feelings, sounds and textures, reflects how Luis Barragán

[72]

[73]

was able to blend memories with endless discoveries; to merge trips, books, friendships, landscapes and different cultures. With Barragán, architecture appears as a natural revelation of recollections and surprise, a central element for elevating quotidian experiences. A statement written in 1985 by Barragán and two friends from his youth, Ignacio Díaz Morales and Rafael Urzúa, composed in their eighties, synthesizes his lifetime dedication to expanding the scope of architecture – and

[28] Raúl Ferrera, *Trabajo con Luis Barragán*, exh. cat. Museo Rufino Tamayo, Mexico City, 1985, p. 30.
[29] Ibid., p. 31.
[30] See Riggen Martínez, *Luis Barragán*, 2000, p. 64.

to redefining it: "This is the great challenge and responsibility of the architect, that his spaces give rise to happiness."[30]

■

[74]

[75]

Captions / Credits

The author expresses special thanks to Guillermo Eguiarte, Director of Casa Luis Barragán in Mexico City, for his gracious and generous support during the extended period of research on site, and for allowing photographs to be taken of the library and its contents.

The illustrations for this publication were compiled by the author and editors. Every reasonable effort has been made to identify copyright owners and to supply complete and correct credits. In the case of errors or omissions, we kindly request that you contact the publisher so that corrections can be addressed in any subsequent edition.

[01]
Luis Barragán in his library, mid 1950s
Magazine cutting (Barragán Archive)

[02]
Luis Barragán, Barragán House at
14 Calle Francisco Ramírez, Mexico City, 1948
Photo Armando Salas Portugal (Barragán Archive)

[03]
Luis Barragán, Barragán House at
14 Calle Francisco Ramírez, Mexico City, 1948
Photo Armando Salas Portugal (Barragán Archive)

[04]
Luis Barragán, Barragán House at
14 Calle Francisco Ramírez, Mexico City, 1948
Photo Armando Salas Portugal (Barragán Archive)

[05]
Luis Barragán in his library, 1963
Photo Ursula Bernath (Barragán Archive)

[06, 07, 08]
Luis Barragán's library, preserved as part of the
Casa Luis Barragán, Mexico City
Photo Fernanda Canales

[09]
View of the Alhambra in Granada

[10]
Luis Barragán on a group tour of the Alhambra
in Granada, 1924

[11]
Le Corbusier and Pierre Jeanneret, Pavillon de
l'Esprit Nouveau, Paris, 1925
© F.L.C. / 2024, ProLitteris, Zurich

[12]
Frederick Kiesler, "City in Space" exhibit, Paris, 1925

[13]
Pascual Bravo, Spanish Pavilion at the Exposition
Internationale des Arts Décoratifs et Industriels
Modernes, Paris, 1925

[14]
Barragán's copy of *Les Colombières* (1925)
by Ferdinand Bac
Photo Fernanda Canales

[15]
Barragán's copy of *Jardins enchantés* (1925)
by Ferdinand Bac
Photo Fernanda Canales

[16]
Émile Bénard, Legislative Palace, Mexico City
(unbuilt project), 1903–1904

[17]
Manuel Amábilis, Mexican Pavilion at the
Ibero-American Exposition, Seville, 1929

[18]
Carlos Obregón Santacilia and Carlos Tarditi, Mexican
Pavilion at the Independence Centenary International
Exposition, Rio de Janeiro, 1922

[19]
Ferdinand Bac, "The Red Garden", plate from
Jardins enchantés, 1925

[20]
Luis Barragán, González Luna House,
Guadalajara, 1928

[21]
Le Corbusier, Villa Stein de Monzie,
Garches/Vaucresson, 1926–1928
© F.L.C. / 2024, ProLitteris, Zurich

[22]
Apartment of Charles de Beistegui, Paris, 1929–1931
Photo Lucien Hervé
© F.L.C. / 2024, ProLitteris, Zurich

[23]
Luis Barragán, Pizarro Suárez House,
Mexico City, 1936–1937
Photo J. Vollmer (Barragán Archive)

[24]
Luis Barragán, travel sketch from *Les Colombières*,
Menton, 1931
(Barragán Archive)

[25]
Barragán's copy of *Vers une architecture* (1923)
by Le Corbusier
Photo Fernanda Canales
© F.L.C. / 2024, ProLitteris, Zurich

[26]
Le Corbusier and Pierre Jeanneret, House at the
Weissenhof Estate, Stuttgart, 1927
© F.L.C. / 2024, ProLitteris, Zurich

[27]
Barragán's copy of the MoMA exhibition catalogue
Modern Architecture (1932)
Photo Fernanda Canales

[28]
Built to Live In by Philip Johnson, published by
the Museum of Modern Art, New York, 1931

[29]
Luis Barragán and Richard Neutra in front of the
Pizarro Suárez House in Mexico City, 1937

[30]
Max Cetto, 1930s

[31]
Luis Barragán, Studio-Apartment Building, Mexico
City, 1939–1940 (collaborating architect Max Cetto)

[32]
Juan O'Gorman, House and Studio for Diego Rivera
and Frida Kahlo, Mexico City, 1931–1932
Photo Luis E. Carranza

[33]
Juan O'Gorman, Project for workers' housing
(unbuilt), 1932
© 2024, ProLitteris, Zurich

[34]
Luis Barragán, Gardens in Avenida San Jerónimo,
Mexico City, 1943–1945
Photo Armando Salas Portugal (Barragán Archive)

[35]
Luis Barragán, Jardines del Pedregal, 1945–1952
Photo Armando Salas Portugal (Barragán Archive)

[36]
Luis Barragán, Barragán House at
20 Calle Francisco Ramírez, Mexico City, 1941–1943
Photo Armando Salas Portugal (Barragán Archive)

[37]
Luis Barragán, Barragán House at
14 Calle Francisco Ramírez, Mexico City, 1948
Photo Armando Salas Portugal (Barragán Archive)

[38]
Armando Salas Portugal, Self-portrait on the roof
terrace of the Barragán House at 14 Calle Francisco
Ramírez, early 1950s
Photo Armando Salas Portugal (Barragán Archive)

[39]
Luis Barragán and Mathias Goeritz in the architect's
studio, discussing a model of the Torres Satélite, c. 1957

[40]
Luis Barragán with Jesús "Chucho" Reyes and the
sisters Ruth and Aline Misrachi, 1950s
(Fundación de Arquitectura Tapatía Luis Barragán)

[41]
Clara Porset, undated photograph taken at her flat in
the Studio-Apartment Building designed by Barragán
in Parque Melchor Ocampo, Mexico City

[42]
Luis Barragán, Prieto López House, Mexico City,
1948–1951
Photo Armando Salas Portugal (Barragán Archive)

[43]
Luis Barragán and Max Cetto, House at
12 Avenida de las Fuentes, Mexico City, 1949–1950
Photo Guillermo Zamora

[44]
Francisco Artigas, Gómez House, Jardines del Pedregal,
Mexico City, 1952
Photo Roberto and Fernando Luna

[45]
Luis Barragán and Max Cetto, House at
12 Avenida de las Fuentes, Mexico City, 1949–1950
Photo Armando Salas Portugal (Barragán Archive)

[46, 47]
Cuadernos de Arquitectura, no. 1, March 1954

[48]
Luis Barragán, Travel sketch from Morocco, c. 1952
(Barragán Archive)

[49]
Gunnar Asplund and Sigurd Lewerentz, Woodland
Cemetery, Stockholm, 1917–1940
(commons.wikimedia.org/wiki/File:Skogskyrkogår-
den_1936.jpg)

[50]
Journal of The American Institute of Architects,
no. 4, April 1952
(Barragán Archive)

[51]
Juan O'Gorman, Gustavo María Saavedra
and Juan Martínez de Velasco, Central Library,
Ciudad Universitaria, Mexico City, 1953

[52]
Alberto Arai, Frontones, Ciudad Universitaria,
Mexico City, 1953

[53]
Capuchin Convent Chapel in Tlalpan,
Mexico City, 1954–1963
Photo Armando Salas Portugal (Barragán Archive)

[54]
Church of San Francisco Javier,
Tepotzotlán, 17th century

[55]
Gálvez House, Mexico City, 1955
Photo Armando Salas Portugal (Barragán Archive)

[56]
Capuchin Convent Chapel in Tlalpan,
Mexico City, 1954–1963
Photo Armando Salas Portugal (Barragán Archive)

[57]
Luis Barragán and Mathias Goeritz,
Torres de Satélite, Greater Mexico City, 1957
Photo Armando Salas Portugal (Barragán Archive)

[58]
Arquitectos de México, no. 27, May 1967
(Barragán Archive)

[59, 60]
Barragán's copy of *Townscape* (1961) by Gordon Cullen
Photo Fernanda Canales

[61]
Barragán's copy of *Le poème électronique* (1958)
by Le Corbusier
Photo Fernanda Canales

[62]
Luis Barragán and Juan Sordo Madaleno, Lomas
Verdes master plan, 1964–1967, photo of a model,
published in *Arquitectos de México*, no. 27, May 1967
(Barragan Archive)

[63]
Installation view of the exhibition "Stairs", MoMA,
New York, October 9, 1963 through December 1, 1963
Photo George Barrows (Photographic Archive.
The Museum of Modern Art Archives, New York)
©2024. Digital image, The Museum of Modern Art,
New York/Scala, Florence

[64]
Barragán's copy of *Architecture Without Architects* (1964)
by Bernard Rudofsky
Photo Fernanda Canales

[65]
Barragán's copy of *The Prodigious Builders* (1977)
by Bernard Rudofsky
Photo Fernanda Canales

[66]
Barragán's copy of *Villages in the Sun* (1969)
by Myron Goldfinger
Photo Fernanda Canales

[67]
Luis Barragán's library, preserved as part of
the Casa Luis Barragán, Mexico City
Photo Fernanda Canales

[68]
Interaction of Color (1963) by Josef Albers
© The Josef and Anni Albers Foundation / 2024,
ProLitteris, Zurich

[69]
Luis Barragán and Andrés Casillas, Cuadra San Cristóbal,
Los Clubes, Greater Mexico City, 1966–1968
Photo Armando Salas Portugal (Barragán Archive)

[70, 71]
Luis Barragán, Gilardi House, Mexico City, 1975–1977
Photos Armando Salas Portugal (Barragán Archive)

[72, 73]
Catalogue and installation view of the Luis Barragán
Retrospective at the Rufino Tamayo Museum,
Mexico City, 1985
(Barragán Archive)

[74]
Library in the Barragán House at
14 Calle Francisco Ramírez, Mexico City, 1970s
Photo Paolo Gasparini (Barragán Archive)

[75]
Luis Barragán on the roof terrace of his house at
14 Calle Francisco Ramírez, 1970s
Photo Paolo Gasparini (Barragán Archive)

Published by the Barragan Foundation, Switzerland,
and the Vitra Design Museum, Germany.

Editing: Barbara Hauss
Design: Thorsten Romanus
Distribution: Pinar Yildiz
Printing: DZA Druckerei zu Altenburg GmbH
Paper: Magno Volume 150 und 250 g/qm
Typeface: ABC Marfa, Stanley, VFutura

Vitra Design Museum
Charles-Eames-Str. 2
D-79576 Weil am Rhein
Germany
verlag@design-museum.de
www.design-museum.de

Barragan Foundation
Kluenenfeldstrasse 20
CH-4127 Birsfelden
Switzerland
info@barragan-foundation.org
www. barragan-foundation.org

Printed and bound in Germany

ISBN 978-3-945852-68-2